From: _____

theCouponCollection™

SOURCEBOOKS, INC.
NAPERVILLE, ILLINOIS

i love
you
mom

{ a coupon gift of love and thanks }

SOURCEBOOKS, INC.
NAPERVILLE, ILLINOIS

Published by Sourcebooks, Inc.
P.O. Box 4410, Naperville, Illinois 60567-4410
(630) 961-3900
FAX: (630) 961-2168
www.sourcebooks.com

ISBN 1-4022-0066-8

Printed and bound in the United States of America
DR 10 9 8 7 6 5 4 3 2

Mom,
just because I love you,

{ let's tell each other our

favorite jokes and laugh together. }

the**Coupon**Collection™

SOURCEBOOKS, INC.®
NAPERVILLE, ILLINOIS

Free Weekend!

{ This weekend, Mom has

no chores or responsibilities. }

theCouponCollection™

SOURCEBOOKS, INC.
NAPERVILLE, ILLINOIS

Mom,
just because I love you,

{ I'll say "She can't come
to the phone right now,
can I take a message?" }

theCouponCollection™

SOURCEBOOKS, INC.™
NAPERVILLE, ILLINOIS

"No Friends Over" Coupon.

{ Self-explanatory! }

theCouponCollection™

SOURCEBOOKS, INC.®
NAPERVILLE, ILLINOIS

Instant Coupon:

{ Ask your father! }

theCouponCollection™

SOURCEBOOKS, INC.®
NAPERVILLE, ILLINOIS

This coupon is good for one week of sibling peace.

the**Coupon**Collection™

SOURCEBOOKS, INC.®
NAPERVILLE, ILLINOIS

This coupon entitles Mom to a

shopping trip

with her best friend.

{ No kids allowed! }

theCouponCollection™

SOURCEBOOKS, INC.®
NAPERVILLE, ILLINOIS

Mom,
just because I love you,

{ I will not need to go the mall for two weeks. }

theCouponCollection™

SOURCEBOOKS, INC.
NAPERVILLE, ILLINOIS

This coupon entitles Mom

to one free hour in a
bubble bath.

theCouponCollection™

SOURCEBOOKS, INC.
NAPERVILLE, ILLINOIS

I Love My Pet Coupon.

Mom, because I love you, I will:

wash the dog, clean the litter box, walk the pet,

_____.

{ fill in the blank }

theCouponCollection™

SOURCEBOOKS, INC.®
NAPERVILLE, ILLINOIS

Instant coupon!

{ Emergency ice cream run! }

theCouponCollection™

SOURCEBOOKS, INC.®
NAPERVILLE, ILLINOIS

Magic Curfew Coupon.

{ Mom doesn't have to be home until _____. }

theCouponCollection™

SOURCEBOOKS, INC.
NAPERVILLE, ILLINOIS

Instant coupon:

{ Put the toilet seat down! }

theCouponCollection™

SOURCEBOOKS, INC.
NAPERVILLE, ILLINOIS

Mom,
just because I love you,

{ I won't pretend I didn't
understand what you told me. }

theCouponCollection™

SOURCEBOOKS, INC.®
NAPERVILLE, ILLINOIS

Mom,
just because I love you,

{ I'll let you teach me how to

use the washing machine. }

theCouponCollection™

SOURCEBOOKS, INC.®
NAPERVILLE, ILLINOIS

Mom,
just because I love you,

{ I'll take the garbage out. }

theCouponCollection™

SOURCEBOOKS, INC.®
NAPERVILLE, ILLINOIS

Instant coupon:

{ Clear the table and wash the dishes! }

theCouponCollection™

SOURCEBOOKS, INC.®
NAPERVILLE, ILLINOIS

Mom,
just because I love you,

{ you can choose my bedtime story tonight. }

theCouponCollection™

SOURCEBOOKS, INC.
NAPERVILLE, ILLINOIS

Mom,
just because I love you,

{ we'll eat at the restaurant you choose. }

theCouponCollection™

SOURCEBOOKS, INC.®
NAPERVILLE, ILLINOIS

Mom,
just because I love you,

{ I'll put away my toys without being asked. }

theCouponCollection™

SOURCEBOOKS, INC.
NAPERVILLE, ILLINOIS

Instant silence!

{ This coupon entitles Mom to peace
and quiet while she reads or naps. }

the**Coupon**Collection™

SOURCEBOOKS, INC.
NAPERVILLE, ILLINOIS

Mom,
just because I love you,

I'll help you dust

(but you get the breakables)!

theCouponCollection™

SOURCEBOOKS, INC.®
NAPERVILLE, ILLINOIS

Blooming Love Coupon!

{ This coupon entitles Mom
to a bouquet of her favorite flowers. }

theCouponCollection™

SOURCEBOOKS, INC.®
NAPERVILLE, ILLINOIS

Mom,
just because I love you,

{ I'll bake you a batch

of your favorite cookies! }

theCouponCollection™

SOURCEBOOKS, INC.
NAPERVILLE, ILLINOIS

This coupon entitles Mom to an uninterrupted afternoon of gardening.

theCouponCollection™

SOURCEBOOKS, INC.
NAPERVILLE, ILLINOIS

Mom,
just because I love you,

{ I'll make sure to wipe my feet
before I come inside all this week. }

theCouponCollection™

SOURCEBOOKS, INC.
NAPERVILLE, ILLINOIS

Get Out of Jail
Free Coupon.

{ Mom gets to disappear and
go wherever she wishes for an hour. }

theCouponCollection™

SOURCEBOOKS, INC.®
NAPERVILLE, ILLINOIS

Girls Night
Out Coupon.

{ Mom, call your girlfriends

and go out for dinner and a movie! }

theCouponCollection™

SOURCEBOOKS, INC.®
NAPERVILLE, ILLINOIS

Mom,
just because I love you,

{ I'll draw a picture just for you. }

theCoupon Collection™

SOURCEBOOKS, INC.®
NAPERVILLE, ILLINOIS

Mom,
just because I love you,

{ let's go to the park and

play on the swings together! }

theCouponCollection™

SOURCEBOOKS, INC.
NAPERVILLE, ILLINOIS

Mom,
just because I love you,

{ please·tell me about the day I was born. }

theCouponCollection™

SOURCEBOOKS, INC.®
NAPERVILLE, ILLINOIS

Mom's My Date Coupon.

{ Let's go somewhere we

both love, just the two of us! }

theCouponCollection™

SOURCEBOOKS, INC.
NAPERVILLE, ILLINOIS

Mom,
just because I love you,

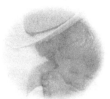

{ let's buy your favorite
      chocolate treat and eat it together. }

theCouponCollection™

SOURCEBOOKS, INC.
NAPERVILLE, ILLINOIS

Mom,
just because I love you,

{ let's go to the zoo and
　　　look at all of your favorite animals. }

theCouponCollection™

SOURCEBOOKS, INC.®
NAPERVILLE, ILLINOIS

Sweetest Smelling
Mom Coupon.

{ Let's go to your favorite
department store and try
on new perfumes together. }

theCouponCollection™

SOURCEBOOKS, INC.®
NAPERVILLE, ILLINOIS

Mom,
just because I love you,

{ let's sing a song together. }

theCouponCollection™

SOURCEBOOKS, INC.®
NAPERVILLE, ILLINOIS

Sweet Tooth Coupon.

{ This entitles Mom to her favorite

sweet treat—sharing it makes

all of the calories disappear! }

theCouponCollection™

SOURCEBOOKS, INC.™
NAPERVILLE, ILLINOIS

Mom,
just because I love you,

{ let's paint pictures of our favorite things. }

theCouponCollection™

SOURCEBOOKS, INC.®
NAPERVILLE, ILLINOIS

Dancing Queen Coupon.

{ Mom, let's put on your
    favorite tunes and dance
        around the living room together! }

theCoupon Collection™

SOURCEBOOKS, INC.®
NAPERVILLE, ILLINOIS

Rainy Day Coupon.

{ Mom, even though it's dreary outside,
let's make hot cocoa and cuddle
on the couch together while we
watch one of your favorite movies. }

theCouponCollection™

SOURCEBOOKS, INC.
NAPERVILLE, ILLINOIS

Mom,
just because I love you,

{ I'll turn down the volume
on my video games. }

theCoupon Collection™

SOURCEBOOKS, INC.
NAPERVILLE, ILLINOIS

Mom,
just because I love you,

{ I'll straighten up my closet
and dresser drawers. }

the**Coupon**Collection™

SOURCEBOOKS, INC.®
NAPERVILLE, ILLINOIS

Wild Card Coupon!

{ Whatever Mom wants, Mom gets! }

the**Coupon**Collection™

SOURCEBOOKS, INC.®
NAPERVILLE, ILLINOIS

Mom's Night Off Coupon.

{ Let's order takeout and eat off paper plates so we don't have to wash them later! }

theCouponCollection™

SOURCEBOOKS, INC.
NAPERVILLE, ILLINOIS

✑ from me to you ✑

I Love You Mom: A Coupon Gift of Love and Thanks

I Love You Dad: A Coupon Gift of Love and Thanks

Dear Grad: A Coupon Gift of Congratulations

Best of Friends: A Coupon Gift of Love and Thanks

Available at your local gift store or bookstore or by calling (800) 727-8866.

Collect them all!

∽ a breath of fresh air ∽

Going Over the Hill Slowly: A Coupon Gift That Keeps You Young
The Wild Side of Womanhood: A Coupon Gift to Unleash Your Audacious Power
Get a Grip: A Coupon Gift to Put You Back in Charge
The Goddess Within: A Coupon Gift that Celebrates You

∽ the country life ∽

I Love You Grandma: A Unique Tear-Out Coupon Gift of Love and Thanks
Dear Mom: A Unique Tear-Out Coupon Gift Just for You
Country Cat: A Unique Tear-Out Coupon Gift for the Feline Lover
A Country Life Wherever You Are: A Unique Tear-Out Coupon Gift for a Simpler Life

Available at your local gift store or bookstore or by calling (800) 727-8866.

Collect them all!

∽ a gift for the spirit ∽

Simple Serenity: A Coupon Gift to Help and Support You
A Little Bit of Feng Shui: A Coupon Gift to Gently Shift Your Energies
A Little Bit of Yoga: A Coupon Gift to Energize and Relax You
Living in Abundance: A Coupon Gift to Enhance and Enrich You

∽ a drop of sunshine ∽

Slow Down: A Book of Peaceful Coupons
Faith, Hope and Love: A Coupon Gift to Restore Your Spirit
Angels: A Coupon Gift of Miracles
The Artist in You: A Coupon Gift to Spark Your Creativity

Available at your local gift store or bookstore or by calling (800) 727-8866.

Collect them all!

theCouponCollection™

SOURCEBOOKS, INC.
NAPERVILLE, ILLINOIS